Living on the Edge:

Preaching Advent in Year C

Living on the Edge:

Preaching Advent in Year C

Parson's Porch
Books
Cleveland, TN

Parson's Porch Books
121 Holly Trail, NW
Cleveland, TN 37311

To order additional copies of this book, contact:

Parson's Porch Books
1-423-475-7308
www.parsonsporch.com

Dedicated to

Dr. Howard Peterson Giddens
November 28, 1910-June 16, 2008

professor, preacher, pastor, mentor, friend, and father

Introduction

This volume contains four sermon series prepared for and preached during the Season of Advent; the sermons are based on the Lectionary texts for Year C.

Advent preaching that grows out of the texts suggested by the Revised Common Lectionary is rewarding in several ways.

First, such preaching underscores our common tradition. The various members, congregations, and denominations that have made up and do make up the Body of Christ in the world share in a common biblical tradition that forms, undergirds, and challenges our faith. At all times, but maybe especially during a special time like Advent, it is exciting for preachers and for congregations to know that we are reflecting together on our common tradition that deals with the sure comings of God into our world and into our midst.

Second, such preaching underscores our common community. Every Sunday we worship in communion with all other Christians who are gathered to worship the God who chose to reveal

God's self most fully and graciously in the person of Jesus Christ, whose coming to Bethlehem's manger, in the Parousia, and to our lives here and now we anticipate during Advent. There is something about a special season like Advent that causes us to appreciate more fully, as we admittedly should all the time, that when we worship God we worship together with all others who worship God.

Third, such preaching underscores our common waiting. We are all in this together. During Advent we are waiting for Christmas but we are also waiting for the Second Coming and we are also waiting for Christ to come to us in whatever new and different ways he wants and needs to come to us and in whatever new and different ways we need him to come to us. In some ways, we will not have to wait long. In other ways, we may have to wait a very long time. Whatever the case, we wait together for Christ to come.

Even so, come, Lord Jesus!

I am very grateful for the congregations of the First Baptist Church of Adel, Georgia, The Hill Baptist Church of Augusta, Georgia, and the First Baptist Church of Fitzgerald, Georgia, in concert with whom these sermons were composed and preached.

Michael L. Ruffin

Part One: Living on the Edge

Living on the Edge of Your Seat
Luke 21:25-36

God is an historical figure; always God has acted in history. From the beginning of the Bible we see him active on earth, working with his human creation. God has always worked in history and has always intervened in historical ways. God is truly an historical figure.

The pinnacle of God's historical activity is the Incarnation. When "the Word became flesh and dwelt among us," when the baby Jesus was born in Bethlehem and was placed in the lowly manger, God put on flesh and walked among us. Never was the historical presence of God clearer than it was then.

It is no great revelation, then, to say that God works in history and works through history. Were it not so we could not know him, for in history is where we live. The question is, how will we live in this history of ours? How will we live in light of the reality of God in our history? How will we live in light of what God has already

11

done and in light of what he will do, insofar as we can understand that?

That was one question among many questions that confronted the disciples of Jesus as he entered the last days of his earthly life. Our passage is the last section of a longer saying from Jesus about the coming of the Son of Man, a phrase that referred to Jesus himself. If you read the entire passage you find that his words about the coming of the Son of Man are set alongside words about the destruction of Jerusalem. The Romans destroyed Jerusalem in 70 AD. Jesus warned his disciples of things that were to happen in just a few years, and he warned them of things that could happen at any time. Some of those things are yet to happen, and some of those things have been happening ever since. All along things happen in history that could be taken as signs that the end is near, but then again most of those things are events that happen in every generation.

We can't even really say that once amazing events happen in nature and in the heavens (vv. 25-27) the time for Jesus' return may be drawing near. After all, Peter had no trouble using words of Joel about such things in his preaching about what had happened at Pentecost (Acts 2:17-21) even though such astronomical tumult did not literally happen when the Holy Spirit fell on the Jerusalem Christians.[1]   Such language is metaphorical language, then. The literal truth is that Jesus will come again some day. The literal truth is that he wants to come to us in new ways today. Sometimes metaphorical language is used to convey that literal truth.

The truth onto which we should hold today is the same truth onto which all Christians in every generation have held. Jesus comes to us in the very day and time in which we live. But one day Jesus will come in a way that is obvious to all and when he does there will be no doubt about it.

In the meantime, Christians should live on the edge of their seats. You know what I mean. You've been to a ball game that was so thrilling that you sat on the edge of your seat, expectantly waiting for what was going to happen next. You've been to a movie that was so enthralling that you sat on the edge of your seat, expectantly watching for the next plot twist. You've read a book that was so engaging that you sat on the edge of your seat, expectantly looking for that next turn of phrase that would make you smile or for the next event that would make you wonder.

Harper Lee's classic *To Kill a Mockingbird* is such a book. In it, we are sort of introduced early

13

on to a character named Boo Radley. I say sort of introduced because we don't see him early in the book. What we have are people's ideas and prejudices and theories about what kind of person Boo Radley might be. He has not, apparently, been outside his family's home for twenty-five years. In various ways the plot revolved around people's conceptions and misconceptions of him. We wonder throughout the pages of the book when he will finally make an appearance and what will happen when he does. It is only in the last few pages of the book that Boo appears and we are not disappointed in the importance of his role. But for well over 200 pages the author keeps you on the edge of your seat, wondering when Boo Radley will show up. That wondering is one of the things that keeps you alert to all the other things that are going on. You truly read on the edge of your seat.

We who are Christians are called to live our lives on the edge of our seat. We are called to live them in a spirit of expectation. One day, you see, Jesus will come back—and it pays to be ready. Jesus warns us here against not being prepared when the day comes. He warns us not to waste our time and our lives in careless, wasteful living. He warns us not to fritter away our time but rather to make good use of the time. He warns us not to get caught up in the momentary distractions of the world. He warns us not to get bogged down by the cares of the world. Their consequence is not eternal and we need to pray for endurance no matter what happens in our life or in our world. We should live ready so that we can be excited about his coming.

We should live on the edge of our seats in another way, too. Remember that the whole occasion of this speech by Jesus was a question about when Jerusalem was going to be destroyed. That event happened some 40 years later, so well within the lifetime of some of his hearers. Even as he was telling them, then, to be ready for his eventual coming, he was also telling them to be ready for ways God was going to act in their own lifetimes. Judgment was coming on Jerusalem. They needed to be ready.

When we know that Jesus is going to return it changes how we live now. It makes us more aware of the ways that he is working in the world right now. Knowing that he will return keeps us in tune with the ways he is moving; it keeps us looking for him so that we see him in the here and now.

Here is the cure for the complacency that some of us feel. Some of us have lost touch with the reality of our relationship with Christ. We forget sometimes that our relationship is with a real Jesus Christ who is a personal figure. He is the Son of God who came and lived among us and then was resurrected. He ascended to be with his Father and he sent his Holy Spirit to indwell us. Through that Spirit we maintain our personal relationship with Christ. And one day he is coming back to claim his Church. And right now he is with us, and right now he works in our lives and in our world. Right now he is calling you to be faithful. Right now he is calling you to be a witness. Right now he is calling you to endure. It is an all-encompassing calling from a surely coming Lord. When he comes, he expects to find us faithful. But even now he comes to us in our lives and calls and enables us to be faithful. When we realize the reality of our relationship with Jesus Christ, how can we help but live on the edge of our seats? How can we help but live with a sense of expectancy over what he is going to do next?

Are you watching? Are you waiting? Are you on the edge of your seat? Or is tomorrow going to be just another humdrum day? When we learn to look for him and to expect him, it changes everything. Let's be people who live on the edge of our seats!

Living on the Edge of a Changed Life
Luke 3:1-6

I wonder for how many of us Jesus is right on the edge of our world, but we have not quite let him come in? How many of us are, consciously or unconsciously, keeping Jesus at arm's length? What difference would it make in our lives if we ever really turn to Jesus? What changes would come to our lives were we really to repent? What change would come about were we to renew our commitment and really follow Jesus?

John the Baptist preached at a time when Jesus was literally about to make his appearance. John was the forerunner to the Messiah, and he was trying to prepare the way for the appearance of that Messiah. And so he used words from the prophecy of Isaiah about the coming of the Lord. He told his listeners that they needed to prepare the way for the coming of the Lord. The "way" that he warned them to prepare was the life that they were living. He summoned them to repent.

They needed to repent, he said, because the Lord was at hand.

The word translated in v. 3 as "repentance" has the literal meaning of "to change the mind." Its meaning goes beyond mere changing of mind or thinking a different way, however. Repentance means to change your mind so that your whole stance toward life changes. You turn around and go the other way. You become a new person. You give up one way to go another way. Of course, you can repent only when the grace of God comes to you. We can repent only because of what God has already done. Nonetheless, repenting is finally something that you have to do; no one can do it for you. But just as it was when John the Baptist preached, if you repent you **will** be forgiven for your sins.

Repentance is more than saying you're sorry, though. Here is where we sometimes make a terrible mistake. We think that if we say we're sorry then God will make everything all right and then once we get over feeling sorry we fall back into a life of disobedience. Sorrow can certainly lead to repentance. But repentance is turning around and going the other way. When you turn to God he takes you and sets you on the path he would have you follow and you go the way he would have you go.

When I was in high school my study Bible was a youth-oriented edition of the Living Bible called *The Way*. In early Christianity the Christian movement was known as "the Way." That's a good way to designate Christian commitment. It is a Way. It is a path taken, a life lived, a road followed. I believe it is still a good word for us to use in describing the commitment we have made. It is the Way. It is the only Way we can live.

The meaning of "repentance" as we are using it then, and as the New Testament often uses it, is really "conversion." As Frank Stagg put it, in the New Testamant,

> *The Greek metanoein literally means 'to change the mind,' but in New Testament usage it includes more, as it calls for a basic change of way....The call to 'repentance,' then, was a call to persons for a radical turn from one way of life to another. In effect it was a call to conversion from self-love, self-trust, and self-assertion to the way of obedient trust and self-commitment to God in Christ as sovereign.* [2]

But such conversion requires that we make the choice to acknowledge that the kingdom is there for us and that God calls us to enter it. John called his listeners to be converted as a way to prepare for the coming of the kingdom, for the coming of the Messiah. Jesus called his listeners to repent because the kingdom of heaven was at hand. Today we call you to repent, to be converted, because the kingdom is right here, the Messiah has come, he is knocking at your door, and he will come again one day. Dallas Willard has offered a simple illustration that might help us to understand the vital truth that to repent means to turn to God, to be converted, and to live his way.

In his childhood Willard lived in a part of southern Missouri where electricity was not available but that changed during his senior year of high school when the Rural Electrification Administration (REA) brought power lines into the area. He observed that, for the residents of his area to take advantage of what the REA had made available, they "had to believe in the electricity" and to take steps to participate in it. Willard concluded,

> *You may think the comparison rather crude,*

and in some respects it is. But it will help us to understand Jesus' basic message about the kingdom of the heavens if we pause to reflect on those farmers who, in effect, heard the message: Repent, for electricity is at hand."

Repent, or turn from their kerosene lamps and lanterns, their iceboxes and cellars, their scrub boards and rug beaters, their woman powered sewing machines and their radios with dry-cell batteries.

The power that could make their lives far better was right there near them where, by making relatively simply arrangements, they could utilize it. Strangely, a few did not accept it. They did not "enter the kingdom of electricity." Some just didn't want to change.

Others could not afford it, or so they thought.3

Change your mind about how to power things and it will change the way that you live! Right here, right now, the kingdom of heaven is at hand. Right here, right now, the Savior is here and he is calling your name. Right here, right now, you are being summoned to repent. Right here, right now, you have the opportunity to be converted. You have the chance to live a changed life. All will be changed if you turn to Jesus and let him change you so that you will live a changed life. But all will remain the same if you keep him at arm's length and don't step over that edge.

Who here needs to repent? Who here is living on the very edge of a changed life? In a sense we all are because we are all sinners. "All have sinned and fall short of the glory of God." To be a sinner means to live life your own way rather than God's way. It means to trust in yourself rather than to trust in God. Some of us have never turned away from that life of sin and turned to God. Some of us have consistently kept Jesus at arm's length. We have heard the message and we have yet to turn to him. We are not yet in the kingdom. Some of us who have never turned to God are living shattered lives. Our lives lie in pieces before us and we're looking for an answer. Repent, be converted, be forgiven, live in the kingdom—that's the answer.

John Claypool told the story of a couple who had a five-year old son. His kindergarten teacher suggested to the class that they make Christmas presents for their parents. The little boy's father smoked a pipe, and he had the idea to make an ashtray for him. So with the teacher's help he molded some clay into a shape approximating that of an ashtray. They painted it blue and put it in a kiln to fire it. The son was very proud of his ashtray. When Christmas pageant night came around the boy excitedly ran to get the wrapped ashtray for his father and in his haste he tripped and dropped the gift. It fell to the floor, and inside the package it broke into several pieces. The boy cried uncontrollably. He had worked so hard and he had so looked forward to his father opening the present on Christmas morning. The father, who was uncomfortable seeing his son cry in public, said, "Don't cry, son, don't cry. It doesn't make any difference." The mother, who knew better, scooped the boy up in her arms saying, "Of course it matters. Now let's pick up the pieces and take them home and see what we can make of what is left."[3]

That is where you may be if you have never turned to the Lord and let him lead you to lead life his way. Your life is in pieces and you wonder if anything can be made of those pieces. The answer is yes. God can make something beautiful of what is left.

Others of you have, somewhere along the way, turned to the Lord and been saved but now you find yourself living far away from him. You are not following the Way as you should and you need a new commitment, a renewed following of the Lord. You have not been living as a kingdom person. You too may be dealing with failure and guilt and disappointment. Are you living on the edge of having a fully changed life? Do you need to return to him today? Do you need a new commitment to the Way? This Christmas needn't be a time of disappointment and disillusionment. It can be a time of change, of conversion, of renewal. What will it be for you?

Living on the Edge of Judgment
Luke 3:7-18

The child had never been to a Christmas service before. When asked what he thought of it, the child said, "I want some of that 'umphant." He was asked what he was talking about. "You know, it's what those people were singing about—'O come all ye faithful, joyful and try 'umphant.' I'd like to try some of that 'umphant.'"[4]

Wouldn't we all! On the Advent calendar today is the Sunday of Joy. We really like to talk about joy at Christmas. And the Bible clearly tells us that Christmas is a time of joy. After all, the angels said to the shepherds that their news was "good tidings of great joy." At this time of year we sing "Joy to the World! The Lord Is Come." All of our "secular" songs encourage us to have joy: "Oh what *fun* it is to ride in a one horse open sleigh"; "Frosty the Snowman was a *jolly happy* soul"; "Then all the reindeer loved him, as they shouted out with *glee*."

Now, though, we interject the voice of the one crying in the wilderness, the prophet John the Baptist. He doesn't say anything like "Don't worry, be happy." He says to get ready because judgment is coming. He says that the judgment has already begun; "the axe is laid to the root of the trees." He says that he has no time for people who want to be baptized just so they can feel like they washed up but who had no real intention of being cleansed. He says that you'd better get your act together because if you don't the judgment is going to be rough. He says a changed life is what God is looking for. And after reporting all these thundering words of warning Luke says something strange about the preaching of John: "So, with many other exhortations, he preached *good news* to the people." Good news! Some of us might say, "With good news like that who needs bad news?"

Fred Craddock has said, "When repentance and forgiveness are available, judgment is good news.... The primary aim is to save the wheat, not to burn the chaff."[5] In other words, the announcement of impending judgment is just plain fact. It is just the truth. It is classified as good news because we still have the opportunity to repent and to be forgiven. The proclamation of judgment tells us that we need to repent and to be forgiven, and that is a truth we need to know. The old saying that says "What you don't know won't hurt you" is not true in this instance.

We need to remember, of course, that John was preaching in anticipation of the appearance of Jesus. His message was that the people needed to get ready because the Messiah was about to come, and when he came the real judgment, the real separation between people, would begin. We live now on the other side of the coming of Jesus, and so we are faced with the need to decide for or against him.

Too many of us are looking for joy in all the wrong places. The voice of John crying in the wilderness tells us that joy is not found in the Band-Aids that we use. Joy is not found in the alcohol that some of us use to lower our inhibitions so that we feel a little giddy. Joy is not found in the mesmerizing influence of hour upon hour of television watching. Joy is not found in the superfluous busy-ness in which many of us immerse ourselves. No! John tells us that joy is found only in facing the truth about ourselves, about God, and about our situation. Joy cannot be found in escapism or in denial. Joy can only be found in hearing the good news about judgment. We are sinners, God judges sin, but there is time to turn to God. There is time to acknowledge the truth and to turn our lives over to him.

Let me be clearer about how living on the edge of judgment can lead to joy. **Joy comes when we rely on a real relationship with God.** Notice that John was not like many modern preachers. When people, even multitudes, came to be baptized by John, he threw up roadblocks. He said, "You brood of vipers! Who warned you to flee from the wrath to come?" (3:7). In other words, he was saying, "You bunch of snakes! Who told you that you could escape God's judgment by just being baptized without really being converted?"[6] He then told them that they needed to bear the fruits that came from repentance. They could not count on their religious heritage.

Today, we need to hear the good news that judgment is coming on those who think that just because they were raised in the church or because Mother and Father went to church that is enough for them. We need to hear the good news that judgment is coming on those who think that just because they went under some water that is enough for them. Now, being raised in church is a good thing. It is better than not being raised in church. Being baptized is a good thing. But neither religious pedigree nor proper ritual will save you. When you realize that and turn to God in truth and in fact, when you give your life over to him, and when he works in your life to convert you, then you are saved. That is good news! And from that real relationship comes real joy!

It is only logical, after all. Think in terms of marriage. My joy in my marriage does not come from the fact that married people raised me. My joy in my marriage does not come from the fact that one day many years ago I said some words and put on a ring, as powerful as those acts were. No, my joy in my marriage comes from my real personal relationship of love, day in and day out, with my wife. Were a married man to find that he did not have that joy because he had never really developed a personal relationship with his wife, that realization would be good news, for then he could be converted and develop that relationship. Impending judgment can give way to glorious joy!

We need to hear something else about how living on the edge of judgment can lead to joy. **Joy comes when our personal relationship with God changes our lives.** John had told the crowd that their heritage was not enough and that if they were baptized without being changed that would not be enough. He talked about producing the right kind of fruit. They asked the question that must be asked when you hear such talk, and it the same question that many of us must be asking right now: "What then shall we do?" (3:10). John replied with assignments that fit with their own particular temptations[7] but which are applicable to all of us. In other words, absolutely every single

34

person who calls herself or himself a Christian ought not to defraud people, ought not to abuse their power, and ought to share with those in need. Period. A Christian businessman should be an honest businessman who would never cheat anyone in any way. A Christian preacher should be a preacher with a keen awareness of the power of the pulpit and should never misuse that power for personal gratification. A Christian person should share out of her abundance with those in need. Each one of us will in addition have our own temptations with which we struggle, and we are to respond as Christ would in all of them.

Make sure that you note, however, that these acts of fruit bearing are the result of a real relationship of faith in God. The acts do not save you; they are the concrete acting out of that relationship of faith. It is true that we are saved by grace through faith and not by works. When you have a real relationship of faith in God that produces joy in your life, one of the avenues for expressing that joy is serving and obeying him. It is true that the grace found in Christ saves us when we trust in him. But will not trust in Christ lead to obedience to Christ? As C. S. Lewis has put it,

> *To trust (Christ) means, of course, trying to do all that He says. There would be no sense in saying you trusted a person if you would not take his advice. Thus if you have really handed yourself over to Him, it must follow that you are trying to obey Him. But trying in a new way, a less worried way. Not doing these things in order to be saved, but because He has begun to save you already. Not hoping to get to Heaven as a reward for your actions, but inevitably wanting to act in a certain way because a first faint gleam of Heaven is already inside you.*[8]

When you realize that judgment is near and is real it is good news because you know that if you are hearing about it there is time to do something about it. What you need to do about it is to turn to God and to enter into a personal relationship with him through his Son Jesus Christ. When you do, you will have a life-changing experience. Not all of the change will happen at once, of course, but it will begin to happen, it will be real, and it will be transforming. It will affect your life at every significant point. The changes will be obvious.

And you will begin to enter into the joy of your salvation.

Living on the Edge of Grace
Luke 1:39-55

Who would want to have been in Mary's place? Her situation could hardly have been more difficult. She was young, she was poor, she was unmarried, and she was pregnant. Up until Gabriel spoke to her, she knew only the first three things, but she knew them well. Her song reveals that she had a clear understanding of her situation in life. It would be saying too much to say that she was a nobody, but it would not be saying too much to say that the world would have regarded her as a nobody. And Mary knew the truth. She knew that everything she was made her weak in the eyes of the world. Yet there was something about Mary. There was something that made her receptive; there was something that made her a willing vessel. For Mary, that something made all the difference.

Something about Mary caused her to be on the edge of grace. What I mean by that is that she was in a position to be the one chosen by God to be the mother of the Messiah. We can only speculate about what caused her to be in that position. We can guess that it had something to do with her upbringing and with her following of God up to that point in her life, but it would only be a guess, and in some ways it would be beside the point. The point is that she was chosen by God to play this great role in his purpose, and that choosing was a matter of God's grace. Surely Mary was a fitting vessel, but the story is not about Mary. It is about God and about what God did. It is about God and what God does.

Mary understood that. By the time she sang her song she had been pummeled with indications that extraordinary things were happening to her. First came that astounding word from the angel: "Behold, you will conceive in your womb and bear a son, and you shall call his name Jesus" (Luke 1:31). That was incredible!

But even more incredible was what Gabriel said to Mary just before that: "Do not be afraid, Mary, for you have found favor with God" (v. 30). Found favor with God! God had seen that something in her, and he had chosen her.

And Gabriel told her that because of that she should not be afraid. It seems to me that being told that you have found favor with God might be reason to be afraid! Why? Because when you find favor with God he does amazing things in your life, and those amazing things bring great responsibility for you great misunderstanding from the world, and potential great heartache into your life. Mary would bear Jesus, she would endure the ridicule of the world and then the persecution of the world. She would raise a son who in his own eyes was more God's than he was hers and who would insist on giving his life away and giving his life away until there was no more life to give, and she would have to stand at the cross and watch him die.

We must tell the truth, though: hearing God's call and doing God's will more than make up for any pain that must be born and any price

41

that must be paid. When you are doing God's will because you know that God in his grace has called you, there is truly no reason to be afraid. Still, Mary said a very brave thing when she said, "Behold, I am the handmaid of the Lord; let it be to me according to your word" (v. 38).

Then there had been the remarkable words of her cousin Elizabeth, who in her advanced age was expecting a baby, too. Listen again to the torrent of exclamations rained down on Mary when Elizabeth first saw her. "Blessed are you among women, and blessed is the fruit of your womb!" (v. 42). "Why is this granted me, that the mother of my Lord should come to me?" (v. 43). "Behold, when the voice of your greeting came to my ears, the babe in my womb leaped for joy!" (v. 44). You can almost imagine Mary having to sit down to catch her breath. First the angel tells her what the Lord is doing in her life, and now Elizabeth, under prophetic inspiration (v. 41) confirms those words. Yes, by the time she broke out in song Mary understood fully that what was happening was all about what God had done and what God would do.

When you realize that the grace of God has touched you, it is time to break out in song, because that is a great way to break out in praise to God. Mary had been touched by the grace of God so she praised God for what he was doing in her life. She praised God for what was happening to *her* because it was in her own life that she experienced God. We also praise God for what he does in our lives. Yet, like Mary, we must be careful how we articulate our praise. Our praise should reflect the way things really are. What God has done in our lives to save us and to use us is not because of our personal merit. It is because of his grace. He has loved us and blessed us and saved us. We must not slip into that deadly trap of thanking God for what he has done for *us*; rather, we must thank **God** for what he has done for us. Don't let yourself think that God has blessed you because of who you are or because of how good you are; all you are really doing then is praising yourself. Our praise is directed to God for what God has done.

Mary praised God for what he had done in her life, and she praised him for doing those things in the life of a person who was among the "lowly" of society. Her lowly state (in terms of the evaluation of the world) put her in a posture to receive what the Lord wanted to do through her. The fact is that only those who have a humble sense of dependence on God are in a position to be used by him. It doesn't matter if no one else thinks that you are usable. It doesn't matter if no one else thinks you're good enough. The decision is up to God; he uses whom he will.

John Kennedy told the story of a Cabinet meeting being presided over by President Lincoln. A question was before the group, and Lincoln said, "All in favor say 'Aye.'" Every member of the Cabinet said "Aye." Then the President said, "All opposed say 'No.'" Then Lincoln and only Lincoln said, "No." The President announced the results: "The vote is 'No.'"[9] You see, the whole world would have voted "No" on Mary, but that didn't matter, because God voted "Yes." The whole world may be voting "No" on you, but that doesn't matter, because God is voting "Yes." And if the whole world votes "No" but God all by himself votes "Yes," then the vote is "Yes."

So Mary was living on the edge of grace when God came to her and blessed her. She accepted that grace and she accepted her place. But this great event was not just for Mary. It was for the whole world; it was for all who would believe. In a sense, the whole world was put on the edge of grace when Mary gave birth to the Christ Child. In the birth of that child the Kingdom of God came, and the opportunity for every person to have God come into their lives was created. Jesus was the culmination of all that God had done with his people throughout their history, and God is still working through Jesus today.

Now, we might think that what happened to and through Mary was a unique event, and in some ways it was. Only Mary gave birth to the Christ Child. Still, I think of a line from the carol "O Little Town of Bethlehem": "O holy Child of Bethlehem! Descend to us, we pray; Cast out our sin, and enter in, Be born in us today!"[10] Christmas is about Christ being born of Mary, but it is also about Christ being born in us. When he comes to us and we accept him, when we say, "Let it be done to me according to your word," then

45

we are saved, and Christ is born in us. Then, we become the instrument of his peace; we become the heralds of his grace to the people who are living right on the edge of accepting it.

Are you living on the edge of grace today? Are you ready to accept Christ? Are you ready to accept the role he has for you to play in his kingdom?

Part Two: The Advent Journey

The Advent Journey:
Toward Right Relationships
Jeremiah 33:14-16; 1 Thessalonians 3:9-13

During this Advent season I want us to think about the Advent journey. The life of faith is a journey. Life with God has its times of tremendous fulfillment. It has its high points. But life with God also has its elements of deep longing and even frustration. We talk a lot about how the birth of Jesus fulfilled hundreds of years of longing by faithful people. We also talk a lot about how we have been waiting now for two millennia for Jesus to come again. But we also go through a lot of yearning and longing in our own lives. And truth be told, as we become more aware of whom God is and of all that he has done, is doing, and will do through his Son Jesus Christ, and as we become more aware of how far this world and we have to go, we will come to yearn and long more and more.

Yet our yearning and longing is not a passive yearning and longing; that is why the metaphor of "journey" is so appropriate. We are to be moving farther down the path that our Lord would have us to follow. Thus I have chosen as the theme verse for this series Psalm 25:5: "Make me to know your ways, O LORD; teach me your paths. Lead me in your truth, and teach me, for you are the God of my salvation; for you I wait all day long." Yes, we wait all day long for God—in fact, we wait all life long—but as we wait we want to know God's ways, we want God to teach us his paths, and we want God to lead us in his truth. We want to know Jesus even while we are waiting for Jesus. We are trusting in his grace for our salvation but we are actively seeking to grow in that salvation so that, when all things are fulfilled, we will stand before him as disciples who have been faithful. And isn't that the goal of the disciple's life—to be found faithful at the end of the journey?

Relationships are vital to life; indeed, relationships comprise a major component of life.

We come into the world in the presence of people: our parents, the doctor, and the nurses; when we take our first breath we take it in the presence of others. It is important that we develop relationships and that we become skilled in having sound relationships. Some of us are more naturally equipped to relate to folks than others. Some people have a very difficult time having healthy relationships. But it is important. And it is very complicated and very difficult. People are very complicated and difficult. You are. I am. We all are! Yet God designed us to live together and to make it through this life together. We are called to work at it.

The goal that Paul set for the Thessalonian Christians is a good goal for us, too. He said, "May the Lord make you increase and abound in love for one another and for all" (v. 12). Such growth in love would be a major way in which they could "be blameless before our God and Father at the coming of our Lord Jesus with all his saints" (v. 13). As we await the Second Coming of Lord, one of our main concerns is that we be ready. We tend to think in terms of morality when we think about being ready, and that is not wrong. Indeed, in the very next paragraph of this letter Paul addresses the fact that growth in holiness has a positive effect on lifestyle in terms of moral and ethical issues. But really, the kinds of things that he talks about there, such as illicit sexual activity that takes advantage of another for personal gratification, would be eliminated if a lifestyle of Christian love was being lived out. Indeed, if we really loved God with all our hearts and if we really loved our neighbor as we do ourselves, that would put an end to all of our moral and ethical problems. But we're not there yet; we have a long way to go.

Paul wanted the Thessalonians to grow in their love for one another. Charity begins at home, they say, and so we need to be always growing in our love for our fellow Christians. Paul spoke of his own love for the Thessalonians and we can use his love as an example of the kind of love for which we should be striving.

First, he said, "Night and day we pray most earnestly that we may see you face to face" (v. 10a). At the time of this writing Paul was in

Corinth, far away from Thessalonica. But he longed to see them and they longed to see him, as Timothy had reported to him (3:6). People who love each other want to be together. So we need to be always growing in our fellowship. We should be grateful when the fellowship of the church is strong. It is good when we hang around and talk with each other after services; it it is good when we disagree with each other at conferences but talk and laugh with each other afterwards; it is healthy we are not separated into a bunch of warring factions. Still, we can always grow in our love and fellowship and we need to do so. Do you need to get to know someone that you don't know? Do you need to get to know someone better? Can we be more involved in each other's lives than we are? It is good if we can be grateful, while still having a long way to go.

Second, Paul prayed that when he saw the Thessalonians he might "restore whatever is lacking in your faith" (v. 10b). I don't think that we should take this in the "when I see you I'll fix what's wrong with you" sense. In fact, to have that attitude toward each other is detrimental to our relationships. Still, Paul was in a position to help them learn and grow in their faith. 1 Thessalonians is probably the earliest writing in the New Testament. Paul was writing to an infant congregation in an infant faith. He was the most learned leader in that new faith. He had a lot to share. In our context, we live 2000 years into the faith and we all have had a lot of opportunities to learn and grow. We have much that we can share with one another. We have differing strengths; we have different areas of expertise; we have varying experiences. Our calling is to contribute to each other's faith; it is to complete one another in the family of faith. We care about each other enough to help each other grow.

Clearly, our human failings make this difficult. Always we need to speak the truth to one another and that can be hard. Our egos make it hard to speak the truth in love; we tend to want to look down on other or to manipulate them or to control them or to hurt them and none of those ways of acting falls under the heading of "love." Our egos make it hard to hear the truth sometimes, even if it is spoken in love and with all good intentions, because we tend to want to get defensive or to adopt a "who do you think you are, you're no better than I am" kind of attitude, when if the person is speaking in love they would readily acknowledge that. Nevertheless, we need to be there for one another, even if being there is difficult or painful.

This love to which Paul calls us, this love that will lead to our having the right kind of relationships, is not to be restricted to our fellow Christians. He said, "May the Lord make you increase and abound in love for one another and *for all.*" God has poured his love into our hearts. His love is not restricted to a few; his love is big enough to be for everybody. Therefore, our love cannot be restricted to a few, either, and we are not allowed to pick and choose who we will love. We are to grow in our love for everybody. God loves them so much that he sent his only Son to seek and to save those who are lost. Do we love them enough to seek them so that God can save them? God loves them so much that he gave his only Son who died on Calvary's cross. Do we love them enough to give ourselves up for them so that they can come to know the Savior who died for them? Jesus went about doing good, healing the sick and restoring the broken. Do we love them enough to emulate his kind of ministry in our community?

Jeremiah and the other prophets looked forward to a time when God's Messiah would come. They looked for that ideal king to bring about a state of justice and righteousness. In shorthand, that means that the relationship between God and people and between people and people would be what it was supposed to be. Of course, there have been in all times people who lived that way; they loved God and they loved others and they tried to show mercy and kindness and to practice justice in every way they could. But when Jesus came, the possibilities increased dramatically, for then the Messiah had come and he had embodied the grace and love of God and he had made it possible for the Holy Spirit to indwell and empower us. In other words, he showed us the way of love and then he equipped us to live in his way of love. One day he will return and then all relationships, like all other realities, will be what they are supposed to be. In the meantime, we have the responsibility and the privilege to grow in our love for one another here within our fellowship and for those out there in that troubling and dangerous world.

We are on a journey with God. As we travel, let's love each other. Let's love others. Let's love more.

The Advent Journey:
Toward Inspired Service
Luke 3:1-6; Philippians 1:3-11

During this Advent season we are talking about being on journey with God. As Christians, we live our lives in light of three comings of Christ: he came to Bethlehem's manger all those years ago, he comes to us in our lives here and now, and he will come again in power. We are awaiting his future Advent but that waiting is active and not passive; in this meantime we want to be learning from God and learning of Christ. The theme verse for my series points us in that direction: "Make me to know your ways, O LORD; teach me your paths. Lead me in your truth, and teach me, for you are the God of my salvation; for you I wait all day long" (Psalm 25:4-5). While we wait we want to be learning and growing. My hope is that this

Advent sermon series will suggest some directions in which we can and should be moving as we learn of and grow in Christ.

Last week I said that our Advent journey can lead us farther down the road toward right relationships. Today I want to say that journey can lead us toward inspired service.

When the Jesus who was born in Bethlehem comes into our lives, he makes a difference. The difference is progressive, that is, he continues to make a difference as we live our lives and that difference should be becoming more and more pronounced. The changes will take place in our souls if they are real changes; they will be internal and not just external. Still, those internal changes will manifest themselves in external ways. So, for example, we will come to have greater and greater love for the people around us and that love will occur at the very depths of our being. We will not just act like we love folks; we will love them in fact. But because we love them in fact we will also show that love in our actions toward them. We serve because we love.

Besides, we are Christians, and we Christians do whatever we do for our Lord. We serve, therefore, because of the way in which our service contributes to the fulfillment of God's purposes in the world. Specifically, we should see our service as preparation for the coming of the Lord. We serve in order to contribute to what God is doing in the world. Christian service is not busywork; we are not to be doing things just to be doing things. Do you remember the bumper sticker that said "Jesus is coming back—look busy"? The thought is all wrong. Jesus is not interested in how busy we look. But he is interested, I believe, in how we are, with changed and changing hearts, living lives that help to prepare the way for his coming.

John the Baptist was the forerunner of Jesus. He preached about the need for people to repent of their sins and to be baptized. In interpreting the work of John the Baptist, Luke quoted from the book of Isaiah.

> *The voice of one crying out in the wilderness:*

> *"Prepare the way of the Lord, make his paths straight. Every valley shall be filled, and every mountain and hill shall be made low, and the crooked shall be made straight, and the rough ways made smooth; and all flesh shall see the salvation of God."*

The quotation is steeped in language that would have made the Israelites remember the exodus from Egypt. The context in Isaiah is the Babylonian Exile; the prophet proclaimed that God was going to come across the desert from Israel to Babylon in order to rescue his people from their captivity. He imagines all the rough places of the wilderness being made smooth and all the winding roads being made straight in preparation for the coming of the Lord to save his people. John was inspired to preach as preparation for the coming of the Lord. He served in order to participate in what the Lord was doing and to help prepare the way for what the Lord was going to do.

We should be inspired to serve, too, because our service is both participation in what the Lord is doing and preparation for what he is going to do. Christian service makes a difference now and it makes a difference for the future. Sometimes we fall into the trap of thinking that the only significant service is that which makes a lot of noise or gets a lot of press or influences a lot of people at once. And, to be sure, what John the Baptist was called to do was big. He and only he was the forerunner of the Messiah. No doubt he was specially equipped by God for the role he was to play. You never know: all of us together or some of us individually may just be called by God to do something big, too. While it is not true that service has to be big and obvious to make a difference, that does not mean that God does not mean for us to do something big and obvious. Never underestimate the power of God to do what needs to be done through us! If there is something huge that God needs accomplished in this community and if God deems that we are the ones to do it, then it is our job to accept the challenge and to go about the task of doing it. If there is a challenging or difficult calling that God places upon your life or my life, then it is our job to, with all the faith we can muster, accept that calling and go about the task of fulfilling it.

Still, it is true that while the seemingly minor or the relatively obscure ways of service may not be seen by some as very significant, in the economy of God they are very valuable. In the New Testament, no one outside of Jesus himself rendered more valuable service than did Paul. Paul did much, sacrificed much, suffered much, and accomplished much. But he could not do what he did by himself; he had to have the support of others. So, in his letter to the Philippians, he said that he always thanked God for them and that he always prayed for them with joy. Why? Because of their "sharing in the gospel from the first day until now" (Philippians 1:5). He furthermore said, "It is right for me to think this way about all of you, because you hold me in your heart, for all of you share in God's grace with me, both in my imprisonment and in the defense and confirmation of the gospel" (1:7). In other words, they had been in the background, encouraging him by supporting his work in practical, tangible ways. In the last chapter of the letter, we learn that he wrote it in order to thank them for a recent gift that they had sent him. Perhaps it was a monetary gift; perhaps it was something else. The bottom line is that they served by helping Paul carry out his ministry. Most of their names are lost to us in the mist of passing time, but every one of them and their congregation as a whole are valuable because of the supporting service they rendered.

Again, I am not willing to let us off the big hook—God may have something he wants us or you or me to do that will require us to be out front and obvious; he may have something major he wants us to do for him. But we need to remember that those checks we write for missions matter. We need to remember that those prayers we pray for missionaries matter. We need to remember that the encouragement we offer to the clerk who waits on us at the grocery store matters. We need to remember that spending one night—just one night—with the guests in the homeless ministry matters. We need to remember that serving on that team that visits shut-ins or nursing home residents or hospital patients or on that team that entertains children so their parents can have a night out or on that team that does odd jobs around a senior citizen's house matters. We need to remember that being there for our hurting brothers and sisters matters. No one act of kindness or ministry may seem all that significant, but in God's big picture, it is.

Does such service do us any good? Of course it does. When it comes from a heart that is being formed into the image of Christ and that is inspired by the love of Christ, of course it does. It does us good right now. It makes us more ready for the coming of Christ, whether that coming is in our hearts in the here and now or whether it is in power in the future. Growing in love in a way that makes us wise and discerning will cause us to live lives that make us ever more "pure and blameless" (v. 10) and loving service will be a large part of such lives. Yes, such service does us a lot of good; it helps to make us into who God intends for us to be and it therefore makes us more and more ready to stand before God.

But such service also paves the way for what God is doing and for what he will do. A Christian is never satisfied with the knowledge that she is being made into a person who is more ready for the coming of Christ; she also wants others to be ready. She wants to do her part in touching others for God and in influencing others with the good news of Jesus Christ. We can't make the world into such a good place that Jesus will return to it. But we can, we should, and we must call as many people to repentance as we can. People need the Lord. We have the Lord. We should be inspired to serve the Lord by serving people; that is how we live out the gospel in these days.

During the 2006 Winter Olympics, I became intrigued by the sport of curling. We don't have much winter here in the Deep South so winter sports seem pretty exotic to me. Curling is kind of like shuffleboard on ice (curlers would not like that characterization, I suspect, but it helps you get the picture if you have never seen the game played). One player slides a large weight called a stone down the ice into the scoring area. It moves very slowly. Two players go before the stone with brooms sweeping the ice; sometimes they sweep feverishly, sometimes they sweep gently, and sometimes they don't sweep at all. It looks like they are trying to get debris out of the way but the main purpose of their sweeping is to create friction that will help to guide the stone. The player who propels the stone down the ice has the most influence over where it will end up but the players who sweep help to steer it along the way to its destination.

We are like those sweepers. We are not in control but we do have a valuable part to play in preparing the way for Christ to come into the lives of the people around us. We do have a valuable part to play in preparing the way for people to be ready when Christ comes in his Second Advent. Our part is to serve by proclaiming the good news, by being out front when we are called to be, and by contributing in the background when we are called to do so.

It is our salvation, our ongoing relationship with Christ, that inspires us. Are we living up to our inspiration? On our Advent journey, are we moving farther down the road toward inspired service?

The Advent Journey:
Toward Real Peace
Luke 3:7-18; Philippians 4:4-7

From my childhood I have loved the hymn "Leaning on the Everlasting Arms." I have especially cherished the line that says, "Leaning, leaning, safe and secure from all alarms." I have always liked and I continue to like the sound of that. I want to be "safe and secure from all alarms." In fact, I would go so far as to say that finding that kind of security has been one of the driving forces in my life. I have always wanted to find real peace and for as long as I can remember I have associated peace with security. That is why, I think, losing both of my parents by the time I was twenty was such a tough experience for me; I had based a lot of my security on the family that I lost.

I am of course not alone in my quest for peace. Real peace is something for which lots of folks are looking. And it's not easy to find. Some of us struggle with situations that cause anxiety to be close at hand and peace to seem out of reach. Most of the time the situations that cause us anxiety and thus rob us of peace are situations that threaten our security. Family issues cause such anxiety. Those issues may arise from situations in the distant past that still have lingering effects or from situations in the present. Often the situations are tied together; hurts from the past influence our present family dynamics and present problems dredge old ones back up. Vocational issues cause such anxiety. We want to know our place in this world. We want to be able to provide for our family. When we struggle over our sense of calling or when our ability to make a living is at risk, our security is threatened and we feel anxious. The realities of the world around us can cause anxiety. The world is a very volatile place. Every community, whether you are talking about a community made up of a few neighbors or a community made up of nations, has within it differences that can lead to tension and even violence. We are all aware that we could be attacked by terrorists or by some rogue state; perhaps our greatest fear is that such a group would acquire and use nuclear or chemical weapons. Our nation is presently involved in protracted conflicts in Iraq and Afghanistan and the expansion of those wars or the development of others is always a possibility.

These and other situations threaten our security and when we feel threatened we feel anxious. Therefore, we seek security so that we can know peace.

Jesus came to this world to make peace possible. "Peace on earth, good will toward men," the angels sang to the shepherds. Paul's words to the Philippians also make that clear. The peace of God, the peace that comes from God, Paul said, will come to those who "rejoice in the Lord," which means not to find your joy in whatever is happening but rather to find your joy in the Lord no matter what is happening. The peace of God, he said, will come to those who let their "gentleness be known to everyone," which means

71

to be able to put up with the slings and arrows sent your way by people because you know that "the Lord is near." The peace of God, he said, will come to those who pray rather than worry. That peace of God, Paul said, "surpasses all understanding"; it is beyond anything we can imagine and it can accomplish far more in our lives than we could ever imagine. And listen to this: from that peace comes security. Paul said that the peace of God "will guard your hearts and minds in Christ Jesus."

That is a revelation to me. I have had it backwards for my whole life. I have lived believing that security would bring me peace. Therefore, I have sought security because I thought that without security I could not have peace. The truth is that without peace I cannot have security. The peace that leads to security comes from living in a personal relationship with Jesus Christ. In fact, peace *is* living in a personal relationship with Jesus Christ. Yes, Jesus came to make peace possible and that peace is ours as we live our lives "in Christ Jesus" (Philippians 4:7). As we live and move and have our being in him, we come to know peace. That peace guards us and keeps us safe; it brings about security.

Security comes from being where you belong; having peace with God creates security because we are where we belong: we are in Christ Jesus. To be in Christ Jesus is to be a part of God's people and to be a part of God's people is to be playing a part in God's purpose.[11] As one of God's people we become members of his community and as community members we have community responsibilities.

For me to have real peace, then, means that I have to move beyond thinking about me. The prophet Jeremiah criticized some of the other prophets of his day for declaring "Peace, peace" when there was in fact no peace. In our approach to the Christian life too many of us settle for less than the real and complete peace that God intends for us to have, I fear. We have entered into a relationship with Christ and so we have peace with God. That gives us security—we therefore don't have to be anxious about our personal situation because we know that our lives and our eternal destiny are in his hands. But peace with

God is meant to lead to peace with other people. Real peace is about God and us, yes, but it is also about us and other people.

Here on the third Sunday of Advent we are confronted with the preaching of John the Baptist. He preached repentance, the need for people to turn from their lives of sin and to turn to God who would forgive their sins. Such repentance leads to a relationship with God that leads to peace. But John was a funny kind of evangelist. Crowds came to him to be baptized and for too many of us that would be enough; crowds are coming to be baptized so the last thing we would want to do is to put up any barriers. Look, though, at what John said: "You brood of vipers! Who warned you to flee from the wrath to come? Bear fruits worthy of repentance" (Luke 3:7-8a). John was telling them that baptism that meant anything would lead to changed lives. Fruits of repentance needed to be evident. And, to their credit, the crowd asked the right question: "What then should we do?" They wanted to know what kind of fruit they were to bear; they wanted to know what their lives should look like if they had truly found peace with God.

John's answers were very pointed and particular. To the crowds he said that they should share out of what they had with those who were in need. To the tax collectors he said that they should not cheat the people from whom they collected taxes. To the soldiers he said that they should not supplement their income by taking advantage of people through the abuse of their power. The actions that would befit repentance always went back in general to treating people like they should be treated. But we all have to apply that general rule to our specific situation.

Repentance of our sins that leads to peace with God should also lead to peace with other people. That is, having a whole, sound relationship with God leads to having whole, sound relationships with other people. Real peace involves all of our relationships. When we operate out of the context of our peace with God that brings about glorious security we have a sound basis for dealing with other people in ways that make for peace.

What would such living look like for you?

Real peace means real change, you see. When you find peace with God it changes the way that you approach and live life and that is why anxiety decreases and security increases. When you find peace with God it changes the way that you approach other people and that is why in our lives generosity should be replacing selfishness, compassion should be replacing judgmentalism, and love should be replacing hate or indifference.

So I ask again, what would such living look like for you? If you are a teacher, what would it mean for you to be so secure in your place before God and in this world that you could give yourself freely to your care and concern for your students? If you are a businessperson, what would it mean for you to be so changed by your relationship with Christ that you would never think of taking advantage of another person for your own benefit? If you are an attorney, what would it mean for you to be so intent on living a life of true repentance that you felt compelled to try to see other people as God sees them? If you are a member of a family, what would it mean for you to be at such peace with God and with yourself that you could deal with your family members with great concern for them and with little concern for yourself?

What I am advocating here today is a movement toward peace in our lives that does not become truncated by our tendency toward self-interest. That is, I don't want us to live satisfied that God has made peace with us and thus our eternal destiny is secured. As valuable as that is, we need to accept the fact that peace with God leads to peace with other people. The Advent journey is a journey toward real peace and that peace will be seen in the way that we relate to others in our every day, workaday lives.

The Advent Journey:
Toward Radical Obedience
Luke 1:39-45; Hebrews 10:5-10

C hristmas is a radical day that commemorates a radical event that was brought about by a radical God who used radical means to bring about a radical result that should inspire radical obedience on the part of his radical followers.

If you will think about what we really celebrate at Christmas you will see the truth of that statement. Christmas is about the eternal Son of God being born in the person of Jesus to the Virgin Mary. It is about the Creator of all that exists being so intent on saving his human creation that he broke into ordinary time and space and dwelled among us. It is about the beginning of the process that would ultimately lead to the cross of Calvary. It is about the birth of the Messiah whose death and resurrection would inspire his earliest generations of followers to risk their lives for his sake.

Why, then, are so many of us so far from being anywhere in the neighborhood of radical in our obedience to God and in our following of Christ? The truth is that even the most committed of us still have a long way to go. In every case—in the case of the marginal disciple, in the case of the lukewarm disciple, and in the case of those trying to be committed disciples—the Advent journey is a journey toward obedient following that is truly radical. We need to move farther down that road and the only day we can begin is today.

The Incarnation itself is an incredibly radical act. The author of Hebrews envisions Christ quoting the words of Psalm 40 and saying, "Sacrifices and offerings you have not desired, but a body you have prepared for me" (Hebrews 10:5). The Son of God was born to Mary and he was a real flesh and blood baby. He grew up to be a real flesh and blood man. Because he was a real flesh and blood man he could die on the cross for our sins. It was a radical way to bring about our salvation but it was God's way. It was "through the offering of the body of Jesus Christ once for all" that "we have been sanctified" (10:10). That means that we have been made holy, that we have been set apart by God to be his servants. We are saved to serve. Given that our salvation came about through such a radical means it stands to reason that our service should be radical as well.

Christ accomplished what he accomplished because he was radically obedient to the will of his Father. Still envisioning Christ quoting from Psalm 40, the author of Hebrews has him say, "See, God, I have come to do your will, O God..." (10:7). All through his life Jesus was dedicated to doing the will of God. No doubt as he grew he became more and more aware of the will of the Father for his life. In the one scene we have from his childhood, Jesus asked his parents if they did not know that he had to be about his Father's business. Throughout his ministry Jesus was determined to live the life that his Father had called him to live and when the end came he was determined to die the death that his Father had called him to die. It was a struggle for him, to be sure; in the Garden of Gethsemane he struggled mightily with his destiny as he asked God to let the cup of suffering pass from him. The struggle ended with the words "Not my will but thy will be done." For Jesus to do God's will required that Jesus practice radical obedience to his Father and that is what Jesus did. As his disciples we want to emulate his radical obedience.

Here is the difficult truth: to emulate the radical obedience of our Savior means to be willing to empty self like he did and to risk all like he did. That is what he told us; he said that those who are willing to lose their lives will find them and that those who take up their crosses and follow him will be his disciples. That is what the Apostle Paul told us; he said that we are to be crucified with Christ and that we are to have the mind of Christ, which he defined as emptying self and becoming a servant. It comes down to this: Jesus poured himself out in obedience to his Father and for the sake of others; as his disciples, we are called to do the same.

What will such radical obedience look like? That will vary from life to life and from person to person. God did not make us all alike and he did not give us all the same abilities and he did not place us all in the same circumstances. Still, some characteristics will apply to the lives of all disciples who move toward radical obedience.

Radical obedience will involve radical love. Jesus loved radically and extravagantly. He loved the outcast and the sinner. He loved the leper and the infirm. He loved those who followed him well and those who did not. He loved people enough to die for them. If we are to practice his kind of radical obedience we will practice radical love. We will be open to all the people around us. We will display grace to everyone we meet. We will confront them with the gospel, with the good news that Jesus came to save sinners, and we will invite them to enter into a relationship with him. We will, if we are to practice radical obedience, love radically and extravagantly. Dying to self and living to God means loving others.

Radical obedience will involve radical forgiveness. Things are not perfect in this world and neither are people. Therefore, we will hurt them and they will hurt us; that's just the way it is. Of course, we should try hard not to inflict pain on someone else. But what do we do when someone else hurts us? Radical obedience to God means offering radical forgiveness to others. Jesus' teachings abound with that instruction. In the Model Prayer, Jesus taught us to pray, "Forgive us our debts as we forgive those who are indebted to us." In that marvelous parable of the unforgiving servant he highlighted the pettiness of someone who has experienced the radical grace of God that has forgiven him an absolutely unpayable debt but who will not forgive someone else's offense against him. Even as he was being nailed to the cross, he prayed, "Father, forgive them, for they know not what they do." We tend to want to say that we are not capable of doing things like Jesus did them and so I have always thought that it was a great gift of God to give us the story of Stephen in the Book of Acts. Stephen was not the Son of God but, when he was being stoned to death, he prayed that same prayer: "Father, forgive them, for they don't know what they're doing." Radical forgiveness is possible for mere mortals who have the Holy Spirit of God in their lives. Dying to self and living to God means forgiving others.

Radical obedience will involve radical service. Christian people, people who have been overwhelmed by the love and grace of God, people who serve the Savior who gave up his place of power in heaven to take on the form of a servant and to serve to the point of death on a cross, come to understand that the way to serve God is to serve others. Giving out of who we are and out of what we have in order to help someone else is just basic Christianity. We tend to want to write people off and to give up on them; we find reasons not to try to help someone who is need. What if God had thought that way? What if God had acted that way? Then we would not be celebrating Christmas because there would be no need; God would not have sent a Savior had God thought like we often do. No, God, out of his abundant love and grace, even though human beings had given him precious little reason to have hope for us, sent his own Son to that manger in Bethlehem and ultimately to that cross on Golgotha. It is the most radical act of help ever extended to undeserving people. How can we help but serve whomever we can in whatever ways we can? Dying to self and living to God means serving others.

I hope that many of us are able to say that we have been making progress in these areas. I hope that we are able to say that our journey with God has already been leading us down the path toward radical obedience. I hope as well that if we can say such things we say them with an appropriate humility that knows that we still have a long way to go. Many of us, though, may realize that we just need to get started. We've been enjoying our salvation but not been doing very much about it. We've accepted the privilege of being saved without taking on much of the responsibility. If that's the case, then the question we might be asking is "Where do we start?"

We start with radical faith. Radical obedience begins with radical faith. Obviously, Jesus had great trust in his Father. But the model I offer to you for this point is Mary the mother of Jesus. When Mary went to visit her cousin Elizabeth, Elizabeth said to her, "Blessed is she who believed that there would be a fulfillment of what was spoken to her by the Lord." It must have been difficult for Mary to believe. The angel Gabriel had come to her and told her that the Lord was with her and that she was going to conceive and bear a son who would be the Messiah and whom she would name Jesus. Mary asked a very good question: "How can this be, since I am a virgin?" The angel answered that it was through the work of the Holy Spirit. Mary's response was and is remarkable: "Here am I, the servant of the Lord; let it be with me according to your word." That is the belief to which Elizabeth was referring. In the moment of crisis and opportunity, Mary had to decide whether or not she believed. She had to decide whether or not she would trust in the power and the promises and the grace of God. She decided that she did, and for her, and in one sense for all of us, that has made all the difference.

And there is where we must start: will we believe? Will we trust? Will we accept that God is God and that Jesus is his Son? Will we accept that when God calls us to radical obedience he really means it and that he has the power to help us live in such obedience? Will we? That is the first step. Do you need to take it?

Part Three: While We Wait

While We Wait: Forgiveness
Psalm 25

Advent is all about waiting. Yet at the same time it is all about fulfillment. At Advent we celebrate what has already happened. What has already happened? Jesus Christ has already come to Bethlehem's manger all those years ago. The baby in that manger became the man on the cross and the man on the cross became our resurrected Lord. Our resurrected Lord will come one day in power to fulfill all the plans and purposes of God. And so we wait. We are waiting for Christmas. We are waiting to experience Christ in a new and powerful way. We are waiting for Christ to come again. We know that God will keep his promises. So we wait but we wait in hope—in biblical hope. Biblical hope is assurance, not wishful thinking. We hope because we know.

In the meantime, though, we sometimes find ourselves, in the words of Ulysses Everett McGill in *O Brother Where Art Thou?*, "in a tight spot." So it was with the psalmist. He found himself surrounded by people who were opposed to him because, so far as he could tell, they were opposed to the real and legitimate ways of God. His situation caused him to turn to God who was, after all, the only one on whom he could really depend. What kind of trouble are you in today? In what kind of tight spot do you find yourself? Look to God. You just might be surprised to find how much power you can find in that tight spot. Herbert O'Driscoll wrote about the Fraser River, which has its beginnings in the mountains of British Columbia and finally empties into the Pacific Ocean. He said,

> *At one stage of that long journey the mountains gather themselves to form a deep narrow canyon through which the Fraser must pass. It does so in a thunderous flood, gouging an almost 200-foot deep bed before spilling into the wide valley that takes it westward to the ocean.*

The river is a word of nature uttering a spiritual truth: Confinement can empower. Confinement can bring into being a bursting-out into wide expanses. John Bunyan in his cell in Bedford, Dietrich Bonhoeffer in his cell at Tegel—they and countless others witness to this truth.[12]

And so in his tight spot the psalmist looked to God. That's where we should look, as well.

He wanted to know the ways of God. That's what we need—to learn of God's ways, of how he would have us to live. He wanted to know the truth of God, because God was the one who had given him salvation. As he waited for what God was going to do, as he waited for the time when his enemies would be dealt with and all things would be made right, he wanted God to remember God's mercy and steadfast love that had always been there for God's people and that would always be there for God's people. But there in his tight spot, there in his time of difficulty, there as he strained and struggled to listen to God and to know God, he had to remember the truth about himself. And so he prayed, "Do not remember the sins of my youth or my transgressions; according to your steadfast love remember me, for your goodness' sake, O LORD!" (v. 7). You see, whether we're in a tight spot or not, honesty should compel us to tell the truth about ourselves. Maybe we're in a tight spot because we put ourselves there. Or maybe we just need to confess the truth. We have sinned against God. We do sin against God.

There is no point denying it. We can't be in the relationship with God that we need if we deny it.

> *A person who owned a Rolls Royce was on vacation when he experienced mechanical failure. He called the company from which he had bought the car, and they flew in a mechanic from England to repair it. After waiting a number of weeks for a bill, the man wrote to the company in England and asked for a bill for fixing the mechanical failure in the Rolls Royce. He received a telex that read, "We have no record of a Rolls Royce with a mechanical failure."[13]*

Sometimes the situations of life or the situations of the world cause us to turn all our attention outward and to ask God to do something about everybody else or about all that. It does us no good to treat our sin like the car company reportedly treated a malfunction in one of our cars. But the truth is that when we honestly ponder the way things are and the way we are we will find that we need to seek and to find the forgiveness of God. This Advent season should be for us all, then, a time for renewed repentance and for the affirmation of our forgiveness.

Jesus Christ was born in the manger. Jesus Christ will return in power. Jesus Christ died on the cross for our sins and was raised on the third day. Now Jesus Christ is with us, challenging us and calling us and convicting us and forgiving us. Our prayer to God needs to be the same as those of the psalmist.

> *For your name's sake, O LORD, pardon*
> *my guilt, for it is great (v. 11).*
> *Consider my affliction and my trouble,*
> *and forgive all my sins (v. 18).*

Honesty compels our confession and repentance. But grace demands it. We are forgiven only because of the wondrous grace of God, grace that was made most evident in what he did in his Son Jesus. How can we not respond to that grace with genuine repentance and with a genuine change of life brought about by the Holy Spirit of God?

Then life can be more like it's supposed to be. Remember: the grace of God is unconditional. The forgiveness of God is because of what Christ did, not because of anything we do. But we must in faith open our lives us to what God wants to do. When we do that, the work begins of being formed to be what God intends us to be. That work continues throughout our lives. Only by living in that continual process can we pray, "May integrity and uprightness preserve me, for I wait for you" (v. 21).

While we wait we find ourselves in a tight spot. In that tight spot we can find power if we'll acknowledge who we are and seek God's forgiveness. Won't you join me this Advent

Season in growing in the grace and forgiveness of our Lord?

While We Wait: Discipleship
Philippians 1:3-11

While we wait for Christ to come back what are we to be up to? We are to be about the business of being disciples of the Christ for whose return we are waiting. Christian waiting is not the twiddling of the thumbs kind of waiting. Christian waiting is rather the having hands that are busy kind of waiting. We really can become and we really should be becoming mature and complete disciples of Jesus Christ.

Ralph Waldo Emerson said, "What lies behind us and what lies before us are tiny matters compared to what lies within us." I think that he meant that what lies in our past and what lies in our future are tiny matters compared to our inner character. We can't quite apply his words to the Advent season; after all, the First Advent that lies behind us and the Second Advent that lies before us are huge events. Still, I want us to focus today on what lies within us. Therein lies the key to becoming the disciples that God has called us to be.

The first thing we need to note is that everything about being a Christian is all about God first. That is good news, because God finishes what God starts. We need to remember that what is happening in us is first and foremost about what God is doing. "I am confident of this, that the one who began a good work among you will bring it to completion by the day of Jesus Christ" (v. 6), Paul said. That is what our life is all about: having God, who began the work of salvation in us, continue to work in and on us all through our lives so that when the end comes we'll be as fully mature as possible. For the most part we settle for far less than that. I wonder why. I wonder if we've never taken God quite as seriously as we should. The truth is, though, that the message of the Bible from beginning to end is that in God we have life and apart from God we have no life. I wonder too if we have taken the "I have been saved" part of salvation very seriously but have failed to take as seriously the "I am being saved" and the "I will be saved" parts. But God is interested in all of it; he wants to keep working on us until the very end.

Perhaps two of the first people to encounter Jesus are good examples for us. When the baby Jesus was forty days old Mary and Joseph went to Jerusalem for Mary's ritual purification and to present the baby to the Lord. There they encountered Simeon. Apparently an old man, he had been looking for what God was going to do to bring salvation to Israel. His heart filled with joy as the Spirit of God led him to the baby Jesus in the temple. Then they encountered a prophet named Anna who was eighty-four and had been a widow for most of her life. She spent virtually all her time in the temple fasting and praying. On that day near the end of her life the Lord let her meet the Messiah, too. Like Anna and Simeon, we can live our lives looking for what the Lord is going to do when he fulfills his promises and along the way we can know his grace and Spirit and presence in ways that make all the difference. It just requires openness and willingness. We are waiting but we are waiting as disciples.

The second thing we need to note is that as maturing disciples the main thing we need to be maturing in is love. Paul said, "It is my prayer that your love may abound more and more...." (v. 9a). The kind of love that Paul names here is *agape*, God's love. The only way that human beings can have *agape* in their lives is if God puts it there. Having that love is one of the basic characteristics of being a Christian. God intends for that love to become an abounding love that grows and grows and grows. What kind of love is *agape*? We learn about it by looking at how God loved us in sending his Son into this world to die for our sin. *Agape* is unconditional love; it is undeserved love; it is selfless love; it is sacrificial love. Have you been growing that kind of love? Are you always becoming a more forgiving person? Are you always becoming a more giving person? Are you always becoming a more sacrificial person? That is what is supposed to be happening. For some reason, though, many people who call themselves disciples of Jesus become less and less open, less and less accepting, and less and less selfless. These things ought not to be. Jesus was born, lived, died, and rose again so that we could, through God's grace and love, become what he intends for us to be. Is that what we're doing?

The last thing I want us to note is that this growing and abounding love is to be an informed and spiritually sensitive love. Paul said that he wanted our love to grow "with knowledge and all discernment, so that you may approve what is excellent, and may be pure and blameless for the day of Christ, filled with the fruits of righteousness which come through Jesus Christ, to the glory and praise of God" (vv. 9b-11). Love does have a point. Our love is not to be aimed into the air randomly; it is be specifically and carefully targeted. It takes a mind that is becoming more and more spiritually discerning to enable us to be appropriately loving. We don't want just to do good things, although doing good things is better than doing bad things. We want to do the best things. And we will know what those are if we are guided more and more by the example of Jesus and by the Spirit of God in our doing them.

As we become, through the grace and love of our Lord, more loving and more other-centered and more sacrificial it will have an effect on us, too. We will become more and ready to stand before our Lord at his Second Advent and to hear him say "Well done." Mike Yaconelli is a name you probably don't know but most youth ministers and lovers of religious satire do. He co-founded Youth Specialties in 1969 and the organization has helped train many people for youth ministry and has provided materials for youth discipleship. He also co-founded the satirical *Wittenberg Door*. In *Messy Spirituality*, a book published first in 2002, he said,

> *I don't want to be St. John of the Cross or Billy Graham. I just want to be remembered as a person who loved God, who served others more than he served himself, who was trying to grow in maturity and stability. I want to have more victories than defeats, yet here I am, almost 60, and I fail on a regular basis.*[14]

Yes, we'll fail. But we can be remembered the ways Yaconelli wanted to be remembered. Perhaps he will; he died in an automobile accident on October 30, 2003.

It is possible. It is more than possible; it is probable. It is more than probable; it is necessary. We can really grow into disciples who, through the grace of our LORD, show more and more love and become more and more ready to stand before God. Don't deny yourself your vital discipleship.

While We Wait: Incarnation
Zephaniah 3:14-20; Isaiah 12:2-6

The Old Testament prophets were usually pointing the people toward better days. Those better days were typically better days for which they would have to wait. The prophets were realists and truth-tellers, though. They did not, like so many now do, just say "everything's going to be all right" or even "everything is already all right." No, they told the truth about justice and judgment. They knew something that too many folks today have chosen to ignore: actions have consequences; if people choose consistently to violate the moral order of God's universe then judgment will come.

But they also knew the truth about God's love, grace, and faithfulness. They knew that God had a day on which he was going to reward his righteous remnant. They knew that in that time

God's people would know forgiveness, security, protection, and vindication. They knew that that wonderful day would be a time to sing and exult and rejoice (Zephaniah 3:14).

Isaiah, prophesying to Judah in the eighth century, and Zephaniah, preaching to that same nation a century later, both knew something else: they knew that the great day of the Lord would be characterized by the presence of the Lord in the midst of his people. Look at what they say: "The king of Israel, the LORD, is in your midst; you shall fear disaster no more" (Zephaniah 3:15b); "The LORD, your God, is in your midst, a warrior who gives victory" (Zephaniah 3:17a); "Shout aloud and sing for joy, O royal Zion, for great in your midst is the Holy One of Israel" (Isaiah 12:6). One of the signs of the presence of the kingdom of God would be the direct presence of God in the midst of his people.

For that day the prophets and the people waited. And so it came to pass that the angel Gabriel paid a visit to a backwater town to a young girl to tell her about the great mess she was about to be in and the great blessing that great mess would be for all the world. The lofty language of the KJV captures it all so well.

> *And the angel came in unto her, and said, Hail, thou that art highly favoured, the Lord is with thee: blessed art thou among women. And when she saw him, she was troubled at his saying, and cast in her mind what manner of salutation this should be. And the angel said unto her, Fear not, Mary: for thou hast found favour with God. And, behold, thou shalt conceive in thy womb, and bring forth a son, and shalt call his name JESUS.... Then said Mary unto the angel, How shall this be, seeing I know not a man? And the angel answered and said unto her, The Holy Ghost shall come upon thee, and the power of the Highest shall overshadow thee: therefore also that holy thing which shall be born of thee shall be called the Son of God.* (L u k e 1:28-31, 34-35)

She was not in this mess alone. So an angel also appeared to Joseph.

*Joseph, thou son of David, fear not to take
unto thee Mary thy wife: for that which is
conceived in her is of the Holy Ghost.
And she shall bring forth a son, and thou
shalt call his name JESUS: for he shall
save his people from their sins. Now all
this was done, that it might be fulfilled
which was spoken of the Lord by the
prophet, saying, Behold, a virgin shall be
with child, and shall bring forth a son,
and they shall call his name Emmanuel,
which being interpreted is, God with us.*
(Matthew 1:20b-23)

Did you catch the phrases? "The Holy
Ghost shall come upon thee." "That holy thing
which shall be born of thee shall be called the Son
of God." "They shall call his name Emmanuel,
which being interpreted is, God with us." There
are other wonderful Scriptures we could quote.
"The Word became flesh and lived among us, and
we have seen his glory, the glory as of a father's
only son, full of grace and truth" (John 1:14
NRSV). "Let the same mind be in you that was in
Christ Jesus, who, though he was in the form of

God, did not regard equality with God as something to be exploited, but emptied himself, taking the form of a slave, being born in human likeness" (Philippians 2:5-7 NRSV). Jesus Christ was God in our midst. Jesus Christ was God with us. Jesus Christ was the incarnate Son of God; he was God in the flesh. Through the Holy Spirit Jesus continues to be in our midst.

How do we live in light of these great truths? One way is by celebrating the truth that God is indeed with us in these days. Remember, we live between the Advents. We look back to the First Advent when Jesus was born in Bethlehem. We look forward to the Second Advent when Christ shall return to fulfill the promises of his kingdom. Still, God is with us right here and right now. We cheat ourselves if we do not grow more and more in our dependence on the power, the comfort, and the instruction of the Holy Spirit.

The other way we celebrate the great truths of the Incarnation is by living out an incarnational ministry ourselves.

We know that we are to be Christ to those around us. We understand that we are the Body of Christ in this world and that if Christ's grace and love are going to be extended to others we are going to have to extend it. And it will be good if we will let other be Christ to us in that same way.

But there is one more angle on this great truth. We are pointed toward it by Jesus' depiction of the last judgment in terms of the separating of people into sheep and goats. Do you remember what he said? The sheep who are put at his right hand are told by Jesus, "I was hungry and you gave me food, I was thirsty and you gave me something to drink, I was a stranger and you welcomed me, I was naked and you gave me clothing, I was sick and you took care of me, I was in prison and you visited me" (Matthew 25:35-36). The righteous want to know when they did any such thing, since one mark of true righteousness is that you don't do your good works to score points with God, and the Lord replies, "Truly I tell you, just as you did it to one of the least of these who are members of my family, you did it to me" (25:40). Reflecting on these powerful words, John Polkinghorne said,

In Advent, we think about the coming of Christ, particularly that first coming at Bethlehem and that final coming at the end of the age to judge the world. But the truth of the matter is that Christ comes to us everyday, anonymously in the people in need who cross our path.[15]

Or as Martin Luther once told his congregation,

There are many of you, who think to yourselves, "If only I had been there! How quick I would have been to help the baby!"... You say that because you know how great Christ is, but if you had been there at that time you would have done no better than the people of Bethlehem.... Why don't you do it now? You have Christ in your neighbor.[16]

So there is a final but certainly not the final twist on the incarnation of Christ. Somehow we must see those people in need around us as our opportunity to minister to Christ. What a

privilege! What a responsibility! What a Savior!
Amen.

While We Wait: Sanctification
Hebrews 10:5-10

Christmas, we say, is the most wonderful time of the year, and in many ways that is true. When I was younger it was also one of the scariest times of the year. I spent a good of time wondering whether I was on the nice list or the naughty list. I usually just wound up hoping that the good things I had done would outweigh the bad things I had done on the great Christmas scale of justice. The wrong-headed question burning in me was "Am I good enough for Christmas to come to me?" Was I good enough for Christmas? What I didn't understand then and what I still don't remember sometimes now is that all that matters is that Christ is good enough. My goodness and your goodness have nothing to do with it. What matters is that Jesus Christ did what he did in order that we might be saved.

Last week we talked about the incarnation. It is so important that Jesus came as a human being with a human body. The author of Hebrews has Jesus reflecting on the words of Psalm 40:6-8 and concluding that God sent him in a body that he had prepared for him in order that he might do the will of God. Only Jesus perfectly did the will of the Father. That perfect obedience led him to sacrifice that body. The sacrifice of Jesus on the cross leads to our sanctification. The work of sanctification has been done once for all in the sacrifice of Jesus' body on the cross. So you see, the coming of Christ at Christmas is vitally important; he came in a body so that he could sacrifice that body for our sins. By his sacrifice we are saved. By his sacrifice we are made holy.

Sanctification is what happens to us because of the sacrifice of Christ. We need to take that truth very seriously. Too often we let ourselves fall into traps. We let ourselves believe that since we're only human no more can be expected of us. We let ourselves believe that since we're no worse than anybody else we know then we're just fine. We let ourselves believe that being a Christian is about following the rules and living a good moral life and so we fall victim to a shallow legalism. But the Bible says that we have been sanctified by the death of Christ. The death of Christ has paid the price for our sins once and for all. The death of Christ has brought us into a direct personal relationship with God. It is the power of God made operative in our lives by the death of Jesus Christ that sanctifies us. So we dare not let ourselves think that we have arrived or that we can't move more and more toward maturity. So to think is to denigrate what Christ did for us. Do we really believe that Christ has changed and is changing our lives? As Dallas Willard put it, "Perhaps the hardest thing for sincere Christians to come to grips with is the level of real unbelief in their own life: the unformulated skepticism about Jesus that permeates all dimensions of their being and undermines what efforts they do make toward Christlikeness."[17]

What does it mean to be sanctified? It means to be made holy. What does that mean? In the Bible being holy means being set apart for

God; it means being set apart for his service and set apart to participate in his covenant. Our sanctification is on the one hand an accomplished fact. It is on the other hand something that is being accomplished in our lives for as long as we live. Surely a major component of being sanctified is that we are becoming more and more like Christ. After all, sanctification means being set apart for God's service and Jesus is the only one who ever got that just right. Only he did God's will just like he was supposed to do. Our goal in life is to become what Jesus was: an absolutely obedient child of God whose only desire is to please our Father and to know and to do his will.

Will we open our lives up to God's grace and love and Spirit and power and wonder? Will we know and live as if we know that God has made us holy and is working to make us holy? Will we let our one desire be to know and to do his will? Will we get to the point in our lives that we are willing to be emptied of self so that we can serve him by serving others? Will we grow and mature to the point that we know that only he knows what it is all about and so we abandon all our little plans into his great plan? Will we get to the point where, when things are bad and times are hard and God seems so very far away that we can pray like our Lord, "Father, if it be possible, let this cup pass from me; nevertheless, not my will but thy will be done"? C. S. Lewis' classic book *The Screwtape Letters* is a fictional record of the letters written by a senior demon named Screwtape to his apprentice nephew demon Wormwood. Screwtape is trying to advise his nephew on how to trip up and mess up a man who has recently become a Christian. In one of those letters he writes,

> *He wants them to learn to walk and must therefore take away His hand; and if only the will to walk is really there He is pleased even with their stumbles. Do not be deceived, Wormwood. Our cause is never more in danger than when a human, no longer desiring, but still intending, to do our Enemy's will, looks round upon a universe from which every trace of Him seems to have vanished, and*

asks why he has been forsaken, and still obeys.[18]

That's a big part of what it is to be sanctified, to be like Christ: no matter what, all we want is to do our Father's will.

Part 4: Advent People

Advent People— Are Longing People
Psalm 25:5; 1 Thessalonians 3:9-13

Our family does not steer in the direction of Christmas until we have arrived safely at Thanksgiving. Only after we make the ten minute drive from Yatesville to Barnesville, ten minutes that pass quickly because we spend them listening to the greatest non-religious Thanksgiving song ever recorded, which of course is "Alice's Restaurant," eat our traditional Thanksgiving meal with my mother's family, stop by to visit my step-brother and step-sister's families, then drive back to Yatesville for the Ruffin family's traditional Thanksgiving bonfire, hot dog roast, and hayride, do we start intentionally listening to Christmas music and plotting our Christmas shopping.

That approach is wise, I think, because once you start giving your attention to Christmas it pulls you forward like a super-magnet. Why? I suspect it is because to our minds Christmas has the potential to bring out the best in people; after all, who could not be at least somewhat affected by all that talk about peace and love and giving? I certainly remember how, when I was a child, the days leading up to Christmas brought out the best in me because I took seriously those rumors about a "naughty and nice" list and didn't want to run the risk of not getting all of the G.I. Joe stuff for which I had asked.

The longing for Christmas, you see, affected my attitude and my behavior—my life—in the meantime.

As strange as it may sound, though, from the Christian perspective it's still not time to turn our full attention to Christmas because on the Christian calendar the Christmas season starts on Christmas Day and extends over the twelve days between Christmas Day and Epiphany. These four weeks leading up to Christmas are known in the Christian tradition as "Advent," a word that means "arrival" and that refers to the arrival or coming of Jesus Christ in at least three ways: (1) his coming all those years ago to Bethlehem's manger, (2) his coming in these days to our lives, and (3) his coming in the future to our world.

These days of Advent, then, are days of longing—we long for the celebration of the birth of Jesus, we long for his second coming and, most significantly for today, we long for his coming to our lives here and now in ways that will affect our attitudes and our behavior—that will affect our lives in the ways that matter the most. We long for his coming to our lives here and now in ways that will form and shape our lives so that the presence of Christ in them will be evident to the people who are around us a lot or who come into our lives for a few seconds.

Paul longed to see the Philippian Christians because he loved them and because he wanted to help them fill up their faith. Paul knew that they, like all Christians in every place and in every time, had a long way to go and he wanted them to get there. Unlike Paul, I am not away from you, but like Paul, I want what is best for you, what is best for all of us; what is best for all of us is that we, here in this time between the first coming of Christ and the last coming of Christ, take full advantage of his coming to us here and now so that we will grow in our faith.

Notice Paul's prayer: "May the Lord make you increase and abound in love for one another and for all, just as we abound in love for you. And may he so strengthen your hearts in holiness that you may be blameless before our God and Father at the coming of our Lord Jesus with all his saints" (vv. 12-13). Paul prayed that the Lord who had been born in Bethlehem, who had died on the cross at Golgotha, who had risen from the dead from the garden tomb, who had ascended to the Father from the Mount of Olives, and who had come to the Philippian Christians' lives to love and save them would work in their lives to make them holy—which means to be useful in God's purpose—and blameless—which means to have matured as they should have—so that they would be ready when the Lord returned.

And what is the essence of being holy, of being blameless, of being ready? It is to "increase and abound in love for one another and for all."[19]

We are Advent people—we long for the celebration of Christmas and for the fulfillment of all things, but let us also long to be all that God means for us to be here and now; let us long to be holy, to be blameless, to be ready—which means to be more and more loving toward each other in the church and toward all those folks out there in the world.

This is a noisy, busy, hectic time of the year. Frederick Buechner, after talking about all the hustle and bustle surrounding Advent, said, "But if you concentrate just for an instant, far off in the deeps of you somewhere you can feel the beating of your heart. For all its madness and lostness, not to mention your own, you can hear the world itself holding its breath."[20]

And that's true—the world and we who live in the world hold our breath in anticipation of what is to come; nonetheless, I want to encourage us to breathe—to breathe regularly, to breathe deeply, to breathe consistently—to feel our breath, to ponder our breath, to increase our breath—and our breath is our love.

Let us pray that we will grow fuller and fuller of God's love that we might love each other more and more. How do we love? That may not be as important as that we love!

One year, a few days before Christmas, my parents and I went to a magical and exotic place called Greenbrier Mall in Atlanta. That particular year, one of the items on my embarrassingly long Christmas list was a toy guitar; being me, I could not make up my mind which of the two models I wanted. The mall had three or four department stores and each one of them had their own stand-in for Santa, who was of course busy at the North Pole making the guitar that I would eventually receive. I went from store to store, constantly changing my mind and constantly letting the next store's Santa know of my change of mind. It didn't really matter, of course, which one I settled on, because either way I would have a guitar; in fact, I do not remember which one I finally received. What does matter, though, is that I never actually learned to play the guitar. It doesn't matter which one I got; it does matter than I didn't use the one I got.

So how do you love? What practices will help us to grow in love? Again, that we love is more important than how we love, but here are some simple suggestions.

Forgive somebody.
Help somebody.
Accept somebody.
Understand somebody.
Visit somebody.

You see, to long for Jesus is to long to live like Jesus would have us live. To long to grow is to long to love. To long to be holy is to long to love. To long to be ready is to long to love.

Look into your heart. For what are you longing?

Advent People— Are Preparing People
Luke 3:1-6

The Advent season, during which we move inexorably and excitedly and apprehensively toward Christmas, is a season of preparation, a time to get ready.

We prepare—we get ready—for Christmas to come by decorating our homes and, if we have company coming, by cleaning them. We prepare—we get ready—for Christmas by making shopping lists of gifts and groceries. We prepare—we get ready—for Christmas at church by hanging the green and by lighting the candles.

While we naturally and appropriately think of Advent as leading up to Christmas, it is of course the coming of Jesus for which we are preparing—and we are getting ready for that coming in all of its aspects: his coming in his birth, his coming in the future, and his coming to us here and now. I want us to think today about getting ready - about being prepared for Jesus to come to us. What should we do—what will we

131

do—to prepare our hearts, our lives, and our church for the arrival of Jesus?

Calling people to prepare for the coming of Jesus was the life work of that wild preacher called John the Baptist. Related to Jesus as kinsman, John's more important relationship to him was as his forerunner, his herald. John went around "proclaiming a baptism of repentance for the forgiveness of sins" and his message was, Luke says, a fulfillment of the prophecy found in Isaiah 40 which said that there would be one "crying out in the wilderness: 'Prepare the way of the Lord, make his paths straight. Every valley shall be filled, and every mountain and hill shall be made low, and the crooked shall be made straight, and the rough ways made smooth; and all flesh shall see the salvation of God'" (3:4b-6). The prophet, who was speaking to Jews in Exile in the 6th century B.C.E., used the image of the way being cleared through the desert for a highway on which God would go to Babylon and take his people home; the prophet also talked about the people getting their lives ready for God's arrival—and that's what John preached about, too.

In a sense, John was making room for Jesus and he was challenging his listeners to make room for Jesus. John's message, as paraphrased by

Frederick Buechner, was "Your only hope...was to clean up your life as if your life depended on it, which it did, and get baptized in a hurry as a sign that you had."[21] And so I say to us today what John said to his listeners: "Get ready because Jesus is coming." "How do we get ready?" you may well ask. John's answer is today's answer: "Repent!"

To prepare for Jesus and to make room for Jesus means to repent and to repent means to change the direction of your life, to turn around and go the other way from the way you have been going. While such turning is finally made possible only by the work of God in our lives, it is nonetheless the case that we must do our part—we must exercise our wills to do those things that make room for Jesus in our hearts and in our midst.[22]

"What things?" you might ask. "How do we need to turn, to change, to repent?" John's listeners asked him the same thing and his answer to them is the answer for us:

> Whoever had two coats must share with anyone who has none; and whoever has food must do likewise." Even tax collectors came to be baptized, and they asked him, "Teacher, what should we do?"

He said to them, "Collect no more than the amount prescribed for you." Soldiers also asked him, "And we, what should we do?" He said to them, "Do not extort money from anyone by threats or false accusation, and be satisfied with your wages" (Luke 3:11-14).

Maybe we cannot be truly open to the coming of Jesus into our individual lives and into the life of the church until we are truly open to the coming of other people into our lives and into the life of the church.

This much is clear from the words of John the Baptist: to get ready for Jesus by repenting means to turn from our unthinking self-centeredness to an intentional focus on the needs of others; to get ready for Jesus by repenting means to turn from our unthinking use and misuse of others for our own benefit to an intentional commitment to do no harm and to do much good; to get ready for Jesus by repenting means to be honest and open and generous and fair and just and righteous and loving in the way we think of ourselves and in the ways we treat others; to get ready for Jesus by repenting means to think of love others like we love ourselves and to act like it.

In his poem "Advent Stanzas," Robert Cording wrote,

> *Each year you are born again. It is no remedy*
>
> *For what we go on doing to each other,*
>
> *For history's blind repetitions of hate and reprisal.*[23]

His coming really is the remedy for such things, of course—the problem is not with him but with us, and the truth is that we have the ability to turn our hearts and lives in the right direction ourselves and then, with his arrival, we will experience the full turning that will make all the difference to those and to those around us.

The hard truth is that all those people who are out there who need so desperately for Jesus to come to them too often cannot see around the curve that we allow—and even cause—to remain in the road rather than straightening it out—by which I mean that we don't straighten our selfishness into selflessness, our greed into generosity, and our cynicism into grace. Once we straighten the way, the prophet said, "all flesh shall see the salvation of God" (v. 6).

John C. Morris tell of a highway in southern Vermont where many serious accidents happen because cars and trucks build up their speed descending a mountain, only to come upon a sharp curve in the road. The people living in the house near that curve keep a pile of blankets on their porch because they know there will be accidents regularly, and the victims will need to be covered while waiting for the rescue squad. Residents of the area have been petitioning the state for years to straighten the road out in order to prevent accidents and save lives. John the Baptist seems to be saying something similar -- the curves of injustice, immorality and inhumanity need to be changed into smooth paths so that everyone will see God's salvation.[24]

I know, I know—we do a lot of things as individuals and through the church to provide blankets to those who need them.

But I wonder: how many people out there can't see Jesus around the curves in the road—around the crooked ways of our hearts, around the distorted ways of our relating, around the graceless ways of our actions—that we refuse to straighten out?

I wonder.

Advent People— Are Rejoicing People
Zephaniah 3:14-20; Philippians 4:4-7

It was in the Children's Sunday School Department weekly assembly at Midway Baptist Church, located four miles outside of Barnesville, Georgia, that I learned to sing it:

> *I've got the joy, joy, joy, joy—down in my heart; down in my heart, down in my heart.*

> *I've got the joy, joy, joy, joy—down in my heart; down in my heart to stay.*

I learned it according to what I heard, though, and what I heard was:

> *I've got the joy, joy, joy, joy—down in my heart; down in my heart, down in my heart.*

*I've got the joy, joy, joy, joy—down in my heart; down in my heart **Tuesday**.*

I couldn't help but wonder—what about the other six days of the week? Why couldn't I have joy on Sunday, Monday, Wednesday, Thursday, Friday, and Saturday?

At some point, of course, I figured out what the song was really saying but that didn't eliminate my question; in fact, my comprehension of the actual words of the song added a question to the one I already had: I now wondered why (1) I couldn't seem to have joy every day of the week—why I didn't have it all the time and (2) why the joy that I did experience didn't seem to have staying power—why it seemed to be fleeting.

I wonder how many of you are wondering those same things. Why can't you have joy all the time? Why can't your joy be the kind of joy that endures?

One truth, of course, is that stuff gets in the way—that life gets in the way.

When the prophet Zephaniah was delivering his message in the second half of the seventh century BCE, the nation of Judah was trying, under the leadership of a good king named Josiah, to find its way out of the moral and spiritual hole into which it had fallen during the long reign of the evil kind Manasseh. Josiah's reign was a time of hope that the people would return to the Lord but the fact was, the prophets knew and said, things would get worse before they got better. Sometimes we look around us and we wonder how the culture of our nation and, for that matter, of the world, got into the shape it is in. We wonder how human life has become so devalued that we accept such things as war, abortion on demand, and sexual promiscuity with nary a second thought. Sometimes we are tempted to put our hope in leaders or in armies or in treaties—and we certainly should hope and pray that such might be of help—but we can't shake the nagging feeling that things will get worse before they get better.

The way that things are in the world gets in the way of a pervasive and permanent joy.

So does the way that things are in our own lives.

Paul encouraged his Philippian sisters and brothers not to worry, which of course means that they were worrying. While he did not say so, his readers knew that Paul had as much or more reason to worry as they did, since he was writing his letter to them from prison. Now, they were worried about things that we have no cause to worry about, given that they were being persecuted for their faith while we are not, but we have things that we can worry about, be it our health, the health of our loved ones, finances, children, parents, grandchildren, vocation—and the list can go on and on. The point is that things in life can make us worry and worry is an impediment to joy.

Neither the things in the world nor the things in our lives that cause us anxiety and that rob us of joy are going to go away; how, then, can we be people who rejoice?

The key is to have our lives get caught up in what God is up to, to have them get caught up in God's actions in the world and in God's attitude toward this world and toward the lives we live in it. God is, as those with eyes to see and ears to hear and faith to believe know, working God's purposes out— and everything really is going to be all right one day. It is not the case that what is going on the world and in our lives is unimportant and insignificant—indeed, God cares very much about all of that and is going to act in judgment and in grace to deal with it all someday; but it is the case that God has greater purposes that will be fulfilled and goals that will be met through and beyond all of that.

In the words of Karl Barth, "In other words, in all that I am, I am only a party to that which God thinks and does. In all that I do, it is not I, but rather God who is important."[25]

And so Zephaniah, after spending many words to make it clear to his listeners that judgment on sin was coming and that it would be so thorough as to seem utter and complete, turned at the end of his message to assure them that on the other side of judgment was salvation, that on the other side of defeat was victory, and that on the other side of devastation was restoration. The prophet proclaimed,

Sing aloud, O daughter Zion; shout, O Israel!

Rejoice and exult with all your heart, O daughter Jerusalem!

The LORD has taken away the judgments against you; he has turned away your enemies.

The king of Israel, the LORD, is in your midst; you shall fear disaster no more. (vv. 14-15)

The people could rejoice because of what the Lord was doing and was about to do; we too can rejoice because of what the Lord is doing and is about to do—but we can also rejoice because of what the Lord has already done. Indeed, we can affirm what Zephaniah said—"The king of Israel, the LORD, is in your midst"—in ways that go beyond what the great prophet knew, because we live on this side of the birth of the baby Jesus who came into this world and into our lives to be the certain presence of the Lord in our midst.

As a part of his message Zephaniah said a very remarkable thing:

> *The LORD, your God, is in your midst…;*
> *he will rejoice over you with gladness,*
> *he will renew you in his love;*
> *he will exult over you with loud singing*
> *as on a day of festival.* (vv. 17-18b)

God rejoiced! God rejoiced, Zephaniah said, over what God was doing to bring about reconciliation, over what God was doing to bring his people back into relationship with him.

Perhaps a joy that can be pervasive and permanent in our lives, a joy that is not contingent on what gains we enjoy or what losses we suffer, a joy that is not dependent on today's circumstances or this moment's emotions, is a joy that is the overflow of what God has done, is doing, and will do through God's Son Jesus Christ.

Zephaniah said that it was a remnant of Israel that would know such joy (3:12-13) but you will remember what the angel said to the shepherds on that night so long ago: "I am bringing you good news of great joy for *all* the people" (Luke 2:10; emphasis added). Yes, it was just a remnant—those few shepherds—who received the good news of great joy that night, but the joy they caught was contagious—it could be caught by all people. Yes, it was just a remnant—those few Wise Men—who were "overwhelmed with joy" when they saw the star over the house where the infant Jesus was (Matthew 2:10), but the joy they caught was contagious—it could be caught by all people.

You see, we can catch God's joy over what God has done, is doing, and will do in Jesus Christ, and others can catch it from us if we will catch it.

It is true that the world can spread despair, but it is more true that God is spreading joy. Which are you catching? Which are you spreading?

Advent People— Are Remembering People
Luke 1:54-55; Psalm 80

I finished writing my Ph.D. dissertation in early 1986; before I could present the oral defense of my work I was required to secure an "outside reader," a scholar in my field from a school other than mine, who would read and render his opinion on those 250 or so pages of blood, sweat, and tears. I was also required to pay that person $500; the problem was that we did not have $500 and had to figure out how to come up with it. My grandfather had recently died and I knew that I would receive some amount of money from his estate but I also knew that the estate was many months away from being settled. So I called one of my uncles who knew the terms of the will and asked if I could borrow the $500 from him and pay it back to him out of my share of the estate; he graciously agreed and I received a compounding of that grace when the estate was settled and my share was reduced by the $500 that I owed him—but no interest had been charged to me!

I have and will always have gratitude for my uncle; I admit also to having felt a little pride in my ingenuity in securing the $500—until, many years later, I was telling that story to a dear friend of many years' standing who said to me, "Why didn't you call us? We would have *given* you the money!"

The answer to the question "Why didn't you call us?" was at least partly pride, of course; I did not want to ask someone for the money who did not have the sure knowledge that I would soon have the resources to repay it. But the other answer to the question was that I did not think of it; it never occurred to me to ask them for help—this despite the fact that they had always given me much help and many resources over the years even though I had not asked for them.

In other words, I failed to remember that they always remembered me, that they always had remembered me and that they always would remember me. In my forgetting I failed to trust in their remembering.

Advent people—people who not only celebrate the coming of Jesus to Bethlehem's manger in the past but who also anticipate his coming to us in the present and to our world in the future—are remembering people, which means that we remember that God always has and always will remember God's people, that God always has and always will remember God's promises, and that God always has and always will remember God's purposes.

Indeed, God's remembering of God's people, promises, and purposes always go together. God is working his purposes out and as God works his purpose out he is keeping his promises and as God works his purposes out and keeps his promises he does so through and with his people.

God's remembering is not at issue—God remembers; but our remembering is an issue—we forget.

Sometimes—all too often, in fact—we forget to remember who God is, what God has done, and what God will do, although our forgetfulness has its roots in what would usually be regarded as understandable circumstances.

One circumstance that affects our remembering is the *passing by of time.*

Mary's song, in which she celebrated the mysterious and wonderful thing that the Lord was doing through her, understood that thing as being a remembrance of God's mercy (v. 54) that was a part of the "promise he made to our ancestors, to Abraham and to his descendants forever" (v. 55). God had made that promise to Abraham some eighteen centuries before Mary sang her song and

147

so, someone might say, God had taken his time in keeping that promise and the truth is that as we reckon time it had been quite a while.

It behooves us to remind ourselves from time to time, though, that God does not reckon time as we do; indeed, one of the many miracles of Christmas is that God, who is eternal and is thus beyond and outside of time, entered this time-bound world in the person of Jesus Christ. For something to be a long or short time to us means little or nothing to God and yet, because he entered our world as one of us, he certainly understands how time is to us and he chooses in his grace to work within the frame of time as we experience it.

It may seem to us sometimes that it is taking a long time for Jesus to intervene in some crisis through which we are going here and now and it may seem to us that it is taking an awfully long time for his Second Advent to occur. We need to remember, though, that Jesus did not come 2000 years ago and never come again; we need to remember that it is not only his Second Coming that counts as an arrival of Jesus in this world. Indeed, Jesus arrives in our world many times over every day—he arrives, just to give one example, when his Body, the Church, exhibits his love and grace and mercy and forgiveness in any real and substantial—in any Christ-like—way.

We need to remember also that, even though Jesus came into our lives when we received him as Savior, his coming to us in whatever crisis we are experiencing now, while it is the next time that we will experience him, is not the only other time that we have experienced him. When we stop and think about it, we will realize that he has come to us many times over as we have needed him, even if we have failed to acknowledge that he was the one who helped. When we stop and think about it, we will realize that he has always been with us and has never forsaken us.

So stop and think about it—how many times did God come to the people of Israel between the promise to Abraham and the coming of Jesus? Psalm 80 talks about God's bringing Israel out of Egypt in the Exodus and the establishment of the nation in the Promised Land, but that's just one occurrence. God's other acts of intervention in the meantime are too numerous to name.

Another circumstance that affects our remembering is the *piling on of problems*. For the Israelites during the time that Psalm 80 was composed and in most of the times during which it was employed in worship, the people were experiencing problems and crises aplenty.

Whether it was occupation, famine, war, or exile, the problems did pile up. Mary praised God for his remembering of his promises and of his mercy during a time when the Romans occupied the land and when she and many like her would have known tremendous struggles in the living of daily life. It would have been easy for Mary and for all of those around her to believe that God had forgotten them.

Sometimes the problems pile up on us, too. We have struggles at work or we have struggles getting work; we have tensions at home; we have sickness in ourselves or in our loved ones; we have grief over the loss of someone or something significant; we have disappointments because someone has let us down or because we have let someone down. The pile of problems is usually partly of our own making and partly of someone else's making and partly of—well, who knows from where some of it comes.

And we get to thinking that God has forgotten. But God does not forget.

God did not forget Israel. God did not forget Mary and her neighbors. And God has not forgotten—and never will forget—us, because God does not forget God's purposes and promises.

The testimony of Mary—the testimony of Advent—the testimony of Christmas—is that God does remember. God does remember God's people, promises, and purposes. Therefore, we can believe, we can trust, we can persevere—we can wait expectantly and actively and creatively.

We can if we will refuse to forget—if we will practice remembering.

So let us remember—let us remember that God remembers; let us remember that the coming of Jesus all those years ago shows just how far God will go to remember his promises so as to fulfill them.

Do you remember? Will you remember?

EndNotes

1

    And that is reported in the other book written by Luke, so he
obviously had no trouble with applying such passages
symbolically to what was literally happening.

2

   Frank Stagg, *New Testament Theology* (Nashville: Broadman, 1962),
pp. 118-119.

3

John Claypool, *Mending the Heart* (Cambridge, MA: Cowley, 1999),
pp. 40-42.

[4] John C. Morris, "Refiner's Fire," *The Christian Century*,
(http://www.christiancentury.org/livingbytheword.html).
5

  Fred B. Craddock, *Luke*, Interpretation Commentary (Louisville:
John Knox, 1990), p. 49.

6

   Cf. I. Howard Marshall, *Commentary on Luke*, New International
Greek Testament Commentary (Grand Rapids:
Eerdmans, 1978), p. 139, for this and other options on
the meaning of John's question.

[7] Craddock, *Luke*, p. 48.

[8] C. S. Lewis, *Mere Christianity* (New York: Touchstone, 1980), pp.
130-131.

9

Theodore C. Sorenson, *"Let the Word Go Forth": The Speeches,
Statements, and Writings of John F. Kennedy* (New
York: Delacorte, 1988), p. 32.

[10] Words by Phillips Brooks.

11

"The kind of prayer Paul urges here restores us to our place as God's
people in God's world for God's purpose. That is the
beginning of shalom." [Earl F. Palmer, *Lectionary*

Commentary: Theological Exegesis for Sunday's Texts, ed. Roger E. Van Harn (Grand Rapids: Eerdmans, 2001), p. 370.]

12

Herbert O'Driscoll, "Pent-up Power," *Christian Century* (November 15, 2003), p. 19.

13

Brian L. Harbour, "The Forgetfulness of God," *Christian Reflection* (2001 Issue entitled "Forgiveness"), p. 50.

14 Michael Yaconelli Messy Spirituality, (Grand Rapids: Zondervan, 2002)pg.19

15 John Polkinghorne, *Living With Hope: A Scientist Looks at Advent, Christmas, & Epiphany* (Louisville: Westminster John Knox, 2003), p. 34.

16 Roland Bainton, *The Martin Luther Christmas Book* (Philadelphia: Westminster, 1948), p. 38, cited in William C. Placher, *Jesus the Savior: The Meaning of Jesus Christ for Christian Faith* (Louisville: Westminster John Knox 2001), p. 57.

17 Dallas Willard, *Renovation of the Heart* (Colorado Springs: NavPress, 2002), p. 88.

18 C. S. Lewis, *The Screwtape Letters* (New York: MacMillan, 1956), p. 47.
19

Cf. I. Howard Marshall, *1 & 2 Thessalonians*, The New Century Bible Commentary (Grand Rapids: Eerdmans, 1983), p. 101: "The purpose or ultimate goal of Paul's prayer is that his converts may be seen as holy at the parousia. The connection of thought makes it clear that this is achieved through growth in love."

20 Frederick Buechner, *Whistling in the Dark: a Doubter's Dictionary* (San Francisco: Harper, 1993), p. 3.

[21] Frederick Buechner, *Peculiar Treasures: a Biblical Who's Who* (San Francisco: HarperCollins, 1979), p. 78.

[22] "Who is going to do this work? It is God's work, but at the same time, it is our responsibility to join that work. That is our work of repentance." [John C. Morris, "Smoothing the Path (Mal. 3:1-4; Lk. 1:68-79; Phil. 1:3-11; Lk. 3:1-6)", *Christian Century*, November 22-29, 2000, retrieved from http://www.religion-online.org/showarticle.asp?title=2011]

[23] Robert Cording, "Advent Stanzas," *The Southern Review*, Spring 2004; reprinted in *The Best American Spiritual Writing 2005*, ed.

Philip Zaleski (Boston: Houghton Mifflin, 2005), pp. 18-22. Used by permission of the author.

[24] Morris, "Smoothing the Path."

[25] Karl Barth, "To Believe," in *Watch for the Light: Readings for Advent and Christmas* (Maryknoll, NY: Orbis, 2001), p. 137.

CPSIA information can be obtained at www.ICGtesting.com
Printed in the USA
244637LV00001BA/9/P

9 781936 912070